Manuel Garcia

Paraguay and the alliance against the tyrant Francisco Solano

Lopez

Manuel Garcia

Paraguay and the alliance against the tyrant Francisco Solano Lopez

ISBN/EAN: 9783743345065

Manufactured in Europe, USA, Canada, Australia, Japa

Cover: Foto ©ninafisch / pixelio.de

Manufactured and distributed by brebook publishing software
(www.brebook.com)

Manuel Garcia

Paraguay and the alliance against the tyrant Francisco Solano Lopez

PARAGUAY

ALLIANCE AGAINST THE TYRANT

FRANCISCO SOLANO LOPEZ.

GENERAL REMARKS--RELIABLE DOCUMENTS.

New York:

HALLET & BREEN, PRINTERS, 60 FULTON STREET.

PARAGUAY

AND

THE ALLIANCE AGAINST THE TYRANT

FRANCISCO SOLANO LOPEZ.

GENERAL REMARKS.—RELIABLE DOCUMENTS.

I.

Public opinion in the United States has been utterly deceived in regard to the intentions of the alliance which for four years has carried on the war against the oppressor of Paraguay. To several causes such a deception may be attributed, and, first of all, to the efforts which Mr. Juan B. Alberdi, a noted supporter of the Paraguayan tyranny, has made in Europe, in order to awaken there, as well as in America, an unfriendly feeling towards the allies, and which have been, to a certain extent, successful, several of the leading journals of the United States, and not a few of its public men, having been led to believe that Paraguay is fighting for freedom and independence. Alberdi is a pamphleteer, *par excellence*, and many are the publications in which he has attempted to prove that the policy now being carried out on the River Plate is exceedingly disastrous. Nevertheless, he was the champion of the same policy in past years when his words were not inspired by strong party feelings and a disappointed ambition. *

---

* In 1852, speaking of Paraguay, this same Alberdi said the following The system of Paraguay is selfish, scandalous, and ruinous to the cause of progress and culture of this part of South America. It deserves the hostility of all patriotic governments. *Bases y puntos de partida :* page 23.

But not only to Alberdi's writings must the present state of public opinion in regard to the Paraguayan question be attributed ; there is another, and a very important cause, and that is, the influence of Lopez' official press upon the American correspondents. It is a well-known fact that the agents of the Dictator have bought the services of several papers in South America as well as those of many of the so-called liberal journals of Europe. The same can be said of Hava's Telegraphic Agency. It is in this manner that calumny has been gaining ground leaving, when unmasked, that *something* which Basilio said always remains, and on which is at present based the mistaken judgment of a large portion of the American people.

But it is time that the real truth should be known. The day has come for the free nations of the world to hurl their curses upon the terrible tyrant whose personal ambition has been the cause of so much bloodshed, and to whom only the desolation of poor unfortunate Paraguay is due. It is necessary that the great American people (and hardly can this people realize the power of tyranny, not having themselves experienced anything of the kind during their independent life) should study the dark pages of Paraguayan history, for then, and only then, will they be able to look in a true light upon the present struggle, its causes, object and probable consequences. This task is not so difficult as it may seem at first sight. The system of government of Francia and both the Lopez, has been, simply, the continuation of the old Jesuitical tutelage of the colonial times, less the pious zeal that tempered the theocratic and irresponsible rule of Loyola's followers.

In no part of the world has the insolent motto of Louis XIV " *l'État c'est moi*" ever offered so practical and constant manifestation as in Paraguay, whose political and social system, is, and always has been, the usurpation of property, and the elimination of the individual, as a citizen and free man to the advantage of the ruler. Under the Jesuits, under Fran-

has been the sole proprietor, merchant and legislator, besides being the obliged father of every family, matrimony itself not being allowed without official consent. The navy of the State has been for years employed in monopolizing the trade of the country. The owners of the valuable woods of that most rich territory have never dared to develop those fountains of wealth, for fear of having their profits confiscated, which would be surely the case, for want of an official permission to that effect. Those who cultivate the *yerba* (Paraguaany tea,) and tobacco—the only branches of industry which are not forbidden—are forced to sell at the prices fixed by the Government, the latter having the right to limit the export of said articles whenever convenient to its own interests. Besides this circumstance, so ruinous to the cultivator, the Government has always regulated the works on the plantations, fixing quantities, extention, &c., with the view of avoiding competence. The Dictator appoints agents or inspectors, whose duty it is to make all persons work for the State, without any compensation whatever, service in the army and navy included.

The Paraguayan policy is opposed not only to emigration, but to any contact with the outside world, probably, through the conviction that the diffusion of general knowledge and liberal ideas would in the end destroy the present political and social system, based, as it is, on selfishness, distrust, and deceit, the true characteristics of that people composed principally of Guaranies, proud as Lopez himself, of their Indian extraction.

II.

At the beginning of the present century the whole of Spanish America, from the River Plate to Mexico, electrified by the ideas originated in North America, and France, during the revolution, raised the flag of independence from the Spanish colonial yoke. The war lasted until 1825, in which year the fields of Ayacucho witnessed the last act of that most glorious epopee. Of all the Spanish American States, the only one that remained indifferent to the struggle between freedom and despotism, was Paraguay, whose Governor, the sole master of the country's destinies, found it convenient to leave to others the hard task of insuring its independence in case of success, undoubtedly, with the intention, should the patriots fail in their attempt, of securing the good will of the Spanish monarch, by making him believe that it was an act of fidelity, what really was nothing but the result of a most criminal selfishness. Such was the policy of Dr. Gaspar A. Francia, of sad memory, who continued in Paraguay the system of patient obedience on the part of the people, of usurpation in every shape, to the advantage of the Government, and of complete isolation from the outside world.

At the death of Francia, in 1840, great hopes were entertained on the River Plate, of a change for the better in the social and political system of Paraguay, but it soon became clear to every one, that his successor, Carlos A. Lopez, would follow in the same path, very likely, because he saw that no people was ever so well prepared for tyranny as Paraguay, organized by means of its Jesuitical institutions, as an immense convent in which individual abjectness was the only law.

Under the name of Consul, a title that Francia had created for himself, Carlos A. Lopez (his nephew) and one M. R. Alonzo, took possession of the Government in 1841, but it did not take the first one very long to get rid of his colleague, and to commence laying the foundation of his dictatorship. To give some appearance of legality to this act, he wrote a Constitution, in which ten years was fixed as the Presidential term, Congress having the power of re-electing the President, by means of a mere formality prescribed in the same Constitution. Everybody may easily understand that a Congress elected by the President, is nothing but an instrument in his hands, whose only duty is to give some legal appearance to his arbitrary acts. It will not be entirely out of place to give here an idea of the so-called Republican Constitution of Paraguay, in order to show how mistaken the American people are when they believe that a Republican form of Government ever existed in that unfortunate country.

Article 1st, very seriously establishes the division of the different branches of the administration, while Article 7th declares that *the authority of the President is unlimited, not only in case of civil and foreign war, but whenever he should deem it necessary for the maintenance of peace and public order.* We leave it to the judgment of our readers so familiar with Republican institutions, to decide what sort of disposition is that which makes the will of one man, the supreme law of the country.

The decennial re-election not being entirely to Lopez' taste, he demonstrated to his pleasing legislators the convenience of establishing a perpetual dictatorship, which was done by act of Congress in 1844. According to the Constitution, Congress can dictate laws, but the President is *de facto*, the only legislator. Congress meets every five years (all powers during its recess residing in the Executive) for the sole purpose of ratifying such acts and dispositions as the Dictator should like to submit. Each session never lasts more than five days, in which time all the acts of the President during the last five years must be examined, the accounts of the administration verified, and such laws as should be thought convenient dictated. We must confess, that to accomplish all this in five days, the Paraguayan Senators and Representatives must require an activity unsurpassed in Parliamentary annals. The sessions are presided over by the President, or one of his delegates, and although the expenses of the administration are to be submitted to Congress, it is understood that they are always *all right.* As a proof of this we may quote here the words of a Paraguayan member of Congress in 1865, " the wealth of the State and that of the President are but one !"

The least opposition in Congress against the President is immediately followed by severe punishment, as was the case in 1842, and 1862, with the members Rivarola and Varela, who dared to pass over the limits prescribed in the President's programme. In 1856 Congress conferred upon the Dictator the right to designate (by secret will) the person who was to succeed him at the head of the Government, a fundamental amendment that was adopted without discussion, and unanimously, as is always the case. A candid member who had played a part in this farce, turned to one of his colleagues and remarked, that he did not think it was worth while to come from so far, on account of such a trifle as the reform of the constitution. The Dictator, who was at the time presiding over the session, heard the remark, and rising from his seat, addressed the imprudent Legislator in the following terms, "You are an insolent man, and a beast, leave the room at once." It is useless to say that the offender availed himself of the advice, and hurried away, terribly frightened.

Another proof of the independence enjoyed by the Paraguayan Legislature is, the *unanimity* with which *all* propositions sent by the President have been, and are always approved. The annals of Parliamentary history in Paraguay do not record a single instance in which a measure advised by the Dictator has been rejected. Of such infallibility not even the Pope can boast.

What we have said of the Legislative Power can be equally applied to the Judicial. Although a hierarchical magistracy exists in name, the President is the private Judge in the cases designated by law, as laying under the jurisdiction of the Judicial Power, and it is exclusively to the Executive that belongs the trial and sentence of all offenders and criminals of a political character. Thus have the Paraguayan Dictators been able to satisfy freely their personal vengeances, disposing at will of the life and honor of the inhabitants of that unfortunate country. Such has been the political life of the tribe which Lopez' admirers have baptized with the sacred name of Republic.

III.

After the fall of Rosas, in 1852, the Argentine Republic recognized the independence of Paraguay, then governed by Lopez I. This one caused the doors of the country to be opened to Argentine commerce, but the Government being the only merchant, it is natural to suppose that the condition of the Paraguayan people was little improved by such a privilege, the Commissioners and Brokers in the service of the Dictator being the only ones to whom the measure proved a fountain of wealth. As to the Paraguayans, they felt happy at being permitted to sell their goods to the Government, by whom the business was looked upon as an inexhaustible mine. Even the hope entertained by some, of Lopez returning to its lawful owners, the property confiscated by his predecessor, was sadly disappointed. Two-thirds of the landed estate of the country belong to this day, to the Government.

Notwithstanding the policy of isolation adopted by the Paraguayan Government, Lopez had in view the conquest at some future day of all the territories that once constituted the Viceroyship of Buenos Ayres. He accordingly proceeded to place the country on a war footing a task not very difficult to accomplish with the power and extensive wealth of the Dictator. He relied upon his two sons, Francisco Solano, and Venancio, to help him in the prosecution of his ambitious plans, and accordingly he gave to the first one the chief command of the armies, and appointed the second, admiral of a few vessels which he pompously denominated with the name of squadron.

Towards the year 1852, the President of Paraguay found it convenient to put himself in contact with Europe, and in consequence, he appointed his son Francisco Solano (general, at the age of 18) Minister Plenipotentiary, and Envoy Extraordinary of Paraguay, near the Courts of France, England and Spain, the same to be accompanied by a numerous suit. This mission gave the following results :—1st. To develop in young Lopez, by means of what he saw in the European Courts, his already boundless ambition. 2d. To sink the future Dictator deep in the mud of Parisian dissipation, and the contraction on his part of habits that afterwards caused the ruin of many a Paraguayan family. 3d. The purchase of war materials in enormous quantities, and the signing of contracts for future remittances. 4th. Lopez' partial instruction in the art of war, especially in regard to fortifications, ordnance, and ammunition, a newly acquired knowledge that made a great impression on his mind, so much as to exclaim, "Once in possession of these means, Paraguay shall be master of the world." 5th. A French decoration.

Carlos A. Lopez' rule ended on the 10th of September, 1862. When he became conscious of his approaching end, he bequeathed to his son, Francisco Solano, the Government of Paraguay, just as if it had been his private property. Congress met in the following month, and as usual, the last act of the Dictator was unanimously approved. "Le roi est mort, vive le roi."

The new ruler commenced his administration under the most favorable auspices. His youth, name, and complete knowledge of his father's policy, together with the superiority which the habits and manners contracted during his residence in Europe gave him, combined to raise him in the estimation, and we may say, admiration of his countrymen. While young Lopez was only a royal prince, or *infante*, he, in immitation of these, surrounded himself with the best educated young men of the country, and succeeded in making them believe that he would not only establish the most liberal reforms, but that he would make himself the champion of a policy far different from that of his father, so jealous and short-sighted. But once at the head of the Government, he made his friends feel how far above them the Dictator of Paraguay was placed. Not a year had elapsed since his inauguration, when he commenced to show his despotic inclinations, as well as a jealousy greater even, than that of his predecessor. Father Maiz, a learned priest, was the first to fall under his rage, and after him, followed many other victims, under pretense of supposed conspiracies, invented by the Dictator in order to enrich himself with confiscated property So true is the fact, that in all times, and in every country, despotism has been the mortal enemy of superiority in any shape, intellectual as well as pecuniary.

The quiet possession of an unlimited power, and the exagerated vanity of the third Dictator of Paraguay, could not but stimulate his ambition. On account of its inland position, Paraguay could not communicate with the outside world without passing through Argentine territory, a circumstance that greatly embarrassed the execution of Lopez' plans. On the other hand, he did not cherish the idea of his subjects becoming acquainted with the social and political condition of their neighbors, the Argentine and Urugayan Republics, and Brazil. All this excited the fiery imagination of the Dictator, who made up his mind to fall in due time upon the adjacent territories with the view of operating by force of arms a radical change in the geography of Paraguay. The ideal of the father became also the ideal of the son, the establishment of an empire on the River Plate was decided upon.

With a perseverance truly *guaraní*, the ambitious Dictator commenced to prepare himself for the crusade. The personel of the army was increased to a number almost incredible, considering the population, * and several men of war were put in readiness by European engineers, who at the same time availed themselves of the topographical position of the country, so admirably adapted for defense, to build formidable fortresses that entirely commanded the River Paraguay and its

---

* Lopez invaded the allied countries with an army of 100,000 men, being a sixth of the total population of Paraguay, and a cipher without precedent in the military history of the world. Six hundred cannon, ammunition enough for a war of ten years, many foreign instructors and engineers, fortifications of every description, and twenty men of war were among the elements with which barbarism intended to overpower civilization. These preparations once made, the Dictator took hold of every male inhabitant from the age of ten to that of ninety years, and who, like the rest, never received any kind of compensation in the way of money, uniform, or sufficient rations.

affluents. Large quantities of war material were stored, the services of experienced officers were secured, and twenty or thirty young men were sent to Europe to study the art of war. The eulogists of Lopez have made a great noise with this seeming act of liberalism, but they have taken good care of saying that although many of these young men distinguished themselves at the examinations, not one of them was allowed to occupy, on his return, the position to which they were entitled by their merit and education. It cannot be said that Lopez used the public money for this laudable pur-. pose, as a forced tax was imposed upon the families of those who had been sent to Europe.

IV.

Two great political parties, the reactionary, and the liberal, or as they are generally called, the *blancos* and *colorados* (white and red) have for many years divided public opinion in the Oriental Republic of Uruguay. In 1864, the blancos succeeded in electing a President from their ranks—Mr. N Aguirre, an opponent of General Venancio Flores, leader of the *colorado* party. This election was the cause of serious disturbances, and the Government being in great need of soldiers, forced many Brazilians into the army, most of them from Rio Grande, a Brazilian Province, bounding with Uruguay. President Aguirre, to whom such outrages were communicated, did not take any step to prevent them, and, in consequence, the Brazilians applied to the Emperor for protection. Justice was not this time denied to them, and a small division of the Brazilian army moved towards the frontier, Mr. Saraiba, the Secretary of the Navy, being at the same time sent to Montevideo to investigate the case, and to demand complete satisfaction, if it was true that Brazilian subjects had been so badly treated. President Aguirre and his Cabinet, to avoid an explanation, maintained that such acts could not be avoided in case of civil war, and the Brazilian Envoy had to retire without obtaining the reparation to which the Empire was so rightfully entitled.

So serious and complicated became the state of the country that General Mitre, the President of the Argentine Republic, and Mr. Thornton, the British Minister, considered it their duty to make an effort in order to bring the contending parties to an agreement. But although General Flores, the liberal leader, showed himself disposed to negotiate, nothing ould be accomplished on account of Aguirre refusing to listen to any peaceful propositions.

New violences having been committed on the frontier of Rio Grande, and several Brazilian Consuls having been insulted by Uruguayan officials, Minister Saraiba sent on the 4th of August, 1864, an ultimatum to the Government, the same that was returned to him on the 9th, accompanied by the following words, " Documents of this sort cannot be kept in the archives of the Oriental Republic of Uruguay." On the following day the Brazilian Envoy left Montevideo to inform his Sovereign that his efforts had been of no avail, and that under the circumstances war was the only means of obtaining justice.

President Aguirre, who had formerly begged in vain for the protection of the King of Italy, threw himself in despair into the arms of the Paraguayan Dictator, to whom he offered in exchange of immediate help, his aid for the occupation of the Argentine island of Martin Garcia, a strong fortress at the mouth of the River Plate, whose possession was very much coveted by the Dictator. The pretext so long expected by Lopez to carry out his ambitious plans of conquest, at last presented itself. And that it was a pretext, the following words quoted from his answer to the Uruguayan Government will fully demonstrate. " On interfering in the question with Brazil, Paraguay *serves its own interests only.*"

Notwithstanding the warlike preparations that had been going on for years in Paraguay, the Dictator lacked the necessary means to attack with any hope of success, the superior fleet of Brazil, and although he could count upon a very strong army, it would have been very dangerous to penetrate into Uruguay, separated as she was from Paraguay by an extensive territory, belonging to the Argentine Republic. Lopez saw this and accordingly made up his mind to wait until everything should be in readiness for a successful invasion. But he did not remain idle. He invaded and took possession of several districts of the imperial province of Matto Grosso, to the north of Paraguay, the same that were sacked with incredible cruelty. In the meanwhile the liberal General Flores, who had conquered his enemies, and afterwards was elected President of Uruguay, proposed to make an alliance with Brazil against the tyrant of Paraguay, an alliance that was immediately accepted. Such was the political situation on the 8th of February, 1865.

V.

What attitude did the Argentine Republic assume under these circumstances ? One of complete neutrality. Paraguay being on the south and east, separated from Uruguay and Brazil by Argentine territory, the Empire sent a Minister to Buenos Ayres to obtain permission for the passage of troops destined to invade Paraguay, and the same was denied by President Mitre on the ground that he was resolved to remain neutral in the struggle. To a similar demand made by Lopez, the same answer was given, and strange as it may appear, this attitude of the Argentine Government, assumed as it was in use of a perfect right of sovereignty, became the Dictator's pretext to invade, on the 13th of April 1865, the Argentine Province of Corrientes. The *guaranies* had entered the war path. The crews of two men-of-war anchored in the bay of Corrientes were decimated, and the city was treated by the unbridled soldiery with as much cruelty as Matto Grosso had been shortly before. ° What could the Argentine Republic do

* On the 5th of March, 1865, a Congress met in Asuncion composed of six hundred members. This numerous assembly of dumb voters remained four

after such provocation, but to accept the challenge and prepare for war ? To act otherwise it would have been necessary to forget what was due to her history and the assailed honor of the National flag.

The government of the three aggrieved nations having the same causes of complaint and the same interests to defend, could not do otherwise than unite in their own defence ; and to that end, on the 1st of May 1865, they entered formaly into a treaty of alliance, which was already in existence " de-facto " owing to the acts of the Dictator Lopez.

The adherents of the Dictator of Paraguay, opponents of the liberal Argentine party, then raised the cry against that treaty ; they appealed to the highest sentiments of patriotism, forgetting in their enthusiasm that the honor of the Argentine Republic was compromised and that no human power could arrest the march of events until reparation should be obtained for the insult offered to the national flag, a reparation so signal as to prevent the repetition of outrages similar to those which commenced the war on the part of the oppressor of Paraguay whose authority, system of government, character and aspirations were at the same time a reproach to America and a constant danger to the liberty of the States adjacent to Paraguay.

The alliance of two Republics with an Empire against a so-called Republic, has awakened the sympathy of this country in favor of Lopez's cause. It has been believed that the influence of the sole Monarchy on the Continent of America, has been at work in the alliance formed against a democratic power ; that the causes of disagreement existing among the Republics have been made use of by that monarchy in order

---

days in session, approving during that time whatever Lopez condescended to propose. The title of Marshall was conferred upon the Dictator. They authorized him to invade Brazil and the Argentine Republic, and finally they enacted several orders of honor to be bestowed upon distinguished individuals with the accustomed crosses, medals &c. The only thing they did of their own accord was an act of menial flatery. The Dictator was recommended not to endanger his precious life during the campaign, a recommendation followed by him *ad pedem literæ.*

to itself take possession of Paraguay. Those who think so forget that Brazil is a power essentially American, a constitutional monarchy with a free government ; they forget that its vast extent of territory could not be increased without great risk to the peace and well being of Brazil and its neighbors. They forget also that Brazil assisted to overthrow the dictatorship of Rosas, and in so doing promoted the establishment of free institutions in the Argentine Republic. They do not stop to study the causes that have irresistibly brought about this war—a war between feudalism and progress ; a war that has grown out of the military and despotic system and ambitious spirit of Lopez, and the geographical position of Paraguay ; a war between monopoly and freedom, between justice and force. The contiguity of a race so widely separated from its neighbors in its habits, traditions, tendencies and language inevitably produced this war, and as inevitably resulted in the alliance between the elements antagonistic to that strange social and political paradox called the Republic of Paraguay.

We believe that the most fastidious person will be entirely satisfied with the context of the treaty of alliance. We will here transcribe literally the main conditions, as they are known to the public, to the end that they may be better understood.

"ART. 6.—The allies solemnly bind themselves not to lay down their arms unless by common consent, nor until they have overturned the actual government of Paraguay [i. e. Lopez]; neither shall they separately treat of nor sign any treaty of peace, truce, armistice or agreement, whatever, to end or suspend the war, except it be mutually agreed to.

ART. 7.—As the war is not waged against the people of Paraguay, but against its government, the allies may admit into a Paraguayan legion all the citizens of that nation who may wish to aid in the overthrow of said government, and will furnish them with whatever they may need, in the form and under the conditions that shall be agreed upon.

ART. 8.—The allies bind themselves to respect the inde-

pendence, sovereignty and territorial integrity of the republic
of Paraguay. In consequence, the people of Paraguay shall
be enabled to choose whatever government and institutions
may suit them, without having to submit, as a result of the
war, to incorporation with any of the allies or having to accept the protectorate of any of them.

ART. 9.—The independence, sovereignty and territorial integrity of the republic of Paraguay shall, in accordance with
the preceding article, be guaranteed collectively by the high
contracting parties for the term of five years.

ART. 10.—It is agreed between the high contracting parties
that the exemptions, privileges or concessions which they may
obtain from the government of Paraguay shall be common to
them all—gratuitously, should they be so obtained, and upon
common conditions, should they be gotten conditionally.

ART. 11.—After the present government of Paraguay shall
have been overthrown, the allies shall proceed to make the
necessary arrangements with the newly constituted authority
in order to secure the free navigation of the rivers Parana and
Paraguay, so that the laws or regulations of said republic
may not obstruct, impede or tax the transit across, or navigation along, said rivers by the merchant or war vessels of the
allied States, bound to points within their respective territories, or within territory which may not belong to Paraguay;
and they shall require proper guarantees to secure the effec-
tiveness of such arrangements, but on condition that such
arrangements concerning river policy—whether as regards the
aforementioned rivers or the Uruguay as well—shall be drawn
up in common accord between the allies and whatever other
littoral States may, within the period agreed upon by the
allies, accept the invitation that may be extended to them.

ART. 12.—The allies reserve to themselves the right of
concerting the most suitable measures to guarantee peace with
the republic of Paraguay after the overthrow of its present
government.

ART. 13.—The allies will, at the proper time, name the
plenipotentiaries who shall represent them in conference to

make whatever agreements, conventions or treaties may be necessary with the new government that shall be established in Paraguay.

ART. 14.—The allies shall exact from said goverment payment for the expenses caused by this war—a war which has been forced upon them; and also reparation and indemnification for the injuries and wrongs done to their public as well as to their private property, and to the persons of their citizens, previous to any express declaration of war; likewise for the injuries and wrongs caused subsequently, in violation of the principles that govern in the laws of war.

The Oriental Republic of Uruguay shall, moreover, exact an indemnity proportionate to the injuries and wrongs which the government of Paraguay hàs done her in this war, into which it compelled her to enter for the defence of her rights, threatened by said government.

ART. 15.—By a special agreement it will be provided for the manner and form of the settlements to be made under the preceding article.

ART. 16.—In order to avoid the discussions and wars which arise out of questions relating to territorial boundaries, it is agreed that the allies shall require of the government of Paraguay to make a special treaty with each one to define their respective boundaries, on the following bases:

The Argentine Republic shall be separated from the Republic of Paraguay by the rivers Parana and Paraguay, up to the point where said rivers touch Brazilian soil, such points, in the case of the Paraguay river, being on its right bank at the Bahia Negra.

The Empire of Brazil shall be separated from the Republic of Paraguay, on the side of the Parana, by the first river below the falls called the Seven Cataracts, which, according to the new map of Manchez,. is the Ygurey, running the line from the mouth of the said river Ygurey, along its whole course to its source. On the left bank of the river Paraguay it shall be separated by the river Apa, from its mouth to its source. In the interior they shall be separated by the Maracajú range of mountains, the eastern slopes of which belong to Brazil, and the western to Paraguay, between the two points at which the shortest straight lines can be drawn respectively from the said range to the sources of the Apa and Ygurey.

Art. 17.—The allies mutually guarantee to each other the faithful fulfilment of the agreements, conventions and treaties that it may be necessary to make with the government that is to be established in Paraguay, in accordance with the stipulations of the present treaty of alliance, which shall remain in full force and vigor until those stipulations be respected and fulfilled by the Republic of Paraguay.

In order to obtain this result they agree that, in case one of the higher contracting parties fails to obtain from the government of Paraguay the fulfilment of its agreement, or that the latter government attempt to annul the stipulations agreed to with the allies, the others shall actively use their efforts to obtain their fulfilment. Should these be useless, the allies shall join together all their means to render effective the stipulations made with them.

Art. 18.—This treaty shall remain a secret until the principal object of the alliance be obtained.

In the stipulations above referred to, there is nothing to excite wonder. It is to the interest of all American nationalities that these stipulations should be fully carried out. By assisting the Paraguayan people to shake off the tyrant's yoke, the allies open to them the way to progress and civilization.

Raising them from slavery, the Allies substitute for the present brutalizing system of servitude, the aspirations of a free people.

There is no design against the independence and sovereignty of Paraguay, the only object being to overthrow a tyrant, whose political existence is inconsistent with this enlightened age.

The aim of the Allies is only to restore the nationality of another American people, giving them the peace and security constantly threatened by the treachery which forms the basis of the policy of the present governor of that Republic,

Neither is there any design of forcing on that people a new government, or of interfering with any form by which they may prefer to be governed.

The independence, integrity, and sovereignty of the Paraguayan people is collectively guaranteed to them in all its plentitude. The allies are not permitted to exercise the least Pretectorate over the Republic as a result of the war. The Allies, far from designing to usurp territories that do not rightfully belong to them, are only defending their own rights, as we shall hereafter show.

VI

Such was the result of the system of equilibrium inaugurated by the Dictator of Paraguay "to restrain the ambitious policy of Brazil," as he said officially, applying to the policy of another goverment, the characteristic of his own. On Lopez rests the responsibility of the bloodshed and the devastation of his country ; they are the fruits of his insatiate ambition for power and his insensate pride. Lopez himself however, has been the providential instrument of his own downfall.

At the outrage of Corrientes a cry of indignation went up from La Plata. The alliance of May 1st was formed, and the Argentine Republic rising from its peaceful state, commenced with all haste her war-like preparations.

Subsequently to the events before mentioned, a Paraguayan division, 12,000 strong, penetrated by way of Rio-Grande to the city of Uruguayana, which they took without resistance on the part of the invaded. This division was defeated by the Allies, without firing a shot, and this commenced a series of encounters which resulted in the evacuation of Corrientes by the invaders, and the protracted and cruel war in Paraguayan territory, a war which with admirable fairness has been presented in the same light as the war in

Mexico during the invasion of the French, and the resistance of Spain against Napoleon I. (*)

This absurd comparison appears in documents proceeding from distinguished officials of the United States, (†) and in

---

(*) What fairness is shown in the comparison made betweeen the cases cited and the situation of Paraguay! In Mexico and in Spain, a foreign power attempted to conquer and seize the soverignty; in the case of Paraguay, on the contrary, the independence of the country is respected, and the object of the alliance is to establish free institutions in a hitherto enslaved country, on the ruins of an unparallelled despotism.

(†) Many rumors and statements are now in circulation tending to create the impresion that the Paraguayans are disheartened and are about to surrender the cause they have hitherto upheld with such admirable courage and perseverance. It may be true that they have lost that "love of liberty that has grown to an overwhelming love of national independence." But unless their minds are completely subdued, there can be no reason for regarding the fall of Angostura and the occupation of Asuncion by the enemy as the conclusion of the war.

It is hardly necessary to revert to the recent events in Mexico, or to the war of the first Empire to show that the military seizure of the capital of an nation does not annihilate its means of resistance, or efface its patriotism, or conclude the war.

If the Paraguayans, retreating to the interior, should still contend for their national life. it will not be by any means the first time in the annals of the Spanish race that a people, overcome by numbers have taken refuge in the mountains, carrying with them their love of liberty and spirit of independence, and have afterwards re-appeared on the page of history with great honor.

The Brazilians will probably be deterred from following the Paraguayans by military and economic considerations. But should the enemy pursue them, the Paraguayans may resort to the means of defence which, in the beginning of the war, they threatened to employ at Itapua on the right bank of the Parana, when the Baron of Porto Alegre encamped at Candelaria, opposite to that place ; they then determined to devastate the land and carry off the cattle as they withdrew before the invaders. Not a living soul was found in Asuncion when the allies took possession of it.

It is very possible that my situation and my interest in the events now occurring in Paraguay may mislead my judgment, but I beg leave to submit to your consideration the propriety of strengthening this squadron by the addition of one or two monitors.

If our government should pursue the same course in this instance as in the case of Mexico, and refuse to recognize the provisonial authorities set up by the invaders, unpleasant contingencies may arise requiring the restraining influence of a superior force.

General McMahon is the only foreign minister residing in Paraguay—his

itself suffices to show how ignorant are its authors as to
the nature of the question between the Dictator of Paraguay and the Allies. These persons and also many distinguished persons in the United States are enthusiastic in their
admiration of the bravery of the Paraguayans, not knowing
that there is a hidden spring that impels them to most extraordinary feats of savage bravery, which indeed would be heroic
if displayed in a cause less disgraced by terror of a despot,
abject submission and the most violent fanaticism. (*) No one
has ever questioned the bravery, the contempt of danger, the
blind obedience which characterized the hordes of Attila, the
followers of Mahomet, or the myrmidons of the Duke of Alva
in Flanders. If mere physical bravery were the test of the
justice of a cause, history would have to reward the meed of
glory to barbarism, and brute force would usurp the place of
right and justice in the annals of mankind. The bravery of
Lopez' soldiers should inspire pity rather than admiration in
the people of a free nation (†), and more especially so when we

conduct and position will be more conspicuous on this account. The press of
the La Plata has already begun to treat him with distrust, and the allies feel
his presence a reproach and a contradiction of their boast that they have overthrown the government of Lopez and captured Paraguay." (Dispatch from
Rear Admiral Davis to the Secretary of the Navy.—January 15th, 1869.)

(*) "It is not" says Minister Washburn, U.S. Minister to Paraguay, "from
extraordinary courage or adhesion to Lopez that the Paraguayan soldier fights
bravely and endures privations. All is due to the military system of Lopez.
To him belongs the honor of the invention: "the soldier never runs less risk
than when marching on to meet the enemy." The Dictator has no confidence
in his army, on the contrary he feels sure of being abandoned as soon as
opportunity occurs. Consequently at each battle the soldiers who stand at the
front are ordered not to give up fighting until they are killed. The second
line is ordered to shoot down every soldier that attempts to flee or to pass
over to the enemy. If these orders are not faithfully executed sentence of death
awaits the delinquents. It is through the fear inspired by these frequent exe-
cutions, that Lopez has been able to form an army composed of men for whom
death has no terrors. When defeated, by reason of superior numbers and consequently forced to retreat, the unfortunate officers are shot and the soldiers
decimated."

(†) It will be well for the reader to become acquainted with the following
facts, that he may fully appreciate the nature of the discipline maintened by

consider what terrible means this cruel tyrant has employed to stimulate his soldiers to resistance, and to punish them when the fortunes of war have been unfavorable to them. (*)

Like the gladiators in the imperial amphitheatres, the Paraguayan armies go submissively to the slaughter, *"morituri te salutant,"* thus proclaiming their Cæsar the supreme master of that unhappy land of walking corpses, where gladness is a thing forgotten, where no emotion dare show itself unless officially authorized. We must repeat, for it cannot be repeated too often, that in this country, where despotism is unknown, it is almost impossible to understand the power of fear and of espionage, the enervation produced by habitual subjection, the paralization of the higher faculties by the continual anguish and apprehension of death, and the dread of impending suffering to those dearest to oneself, every person being held responsible for the faults of his friends, his relatives and his comrades. It is on this non-comprehension in the United States of the meaning of despotism, that the apologists of Paraguay rely; but, in return, we denounce to the civilized world the incredible crimes committed by Lopez in his terrible tyranny over Paraguay. We close this work with documents which were found in the camp of that tyrant, whose cruelty and blood-thirstiness are equal to anything that can be found in the most horrible pages of history.

---

the Dictator. General Robles commanded the Paraguayan army which invaded Corrientes. Hearing that an entire division of his army (12,000) had been killed or taken prisoners, he retreated to Paraguay, to escape the same fate. When he arrived at head-quarters, the Dictator ordered him to be shot, with the further order that two thousand men should fire on him at the same time, with the view of striking a wholesome terror into the hearts of the soldiers thus compelled to fire on their commander. By this act one man was killed and two thousand men left half dead . . . . with terror. (*Revelations on the Paraguayan War*, New York, 1866.)

(*) Lopez has executed not only defeated generals, but also their wives, as in the case of Martinez, the defender of Humaitá.

VII.

We would not consider our task faithfully accomplished had we not shown that the fall of the tyrant of Paraguay is equivalent to the moral, intellectual and material regeneration of the Guaraní race—that unhappy people who have been fossilized by a despotism springing from the Jesuitical hierarchy, under which all freedom of thought, all notions of right, were crushed out. A new condition of things will be favorable to Bolivia, interested, as she is, in the free navigation of the only outlet which her products can have to the Atlantic. It will be favorable to Brazil and the Republics of the Plata, and, in general, to the commerce of the world. The emigration which will be carried thither by liberal laws, will promote the progress and improvement of a race hitherto condemned to the abject subjection and torpor enforced by absolute dynasties.

The friends of Dictator Lopez are those who are opposed to the liberal institutions so ardently desired by enlightened Paraguayans, and upheld by the Alliance. The Alliance is itself interested, for its own security and convenience, in seeing the fall of the monstrous government of the falsely-called Republic of Paraguay. The United States cannot oppose this liberal regeneration, because such opposition is forbidden by their own antecedents and policy, by their desire to widen the moral influence of republican institutions on the American Continent, and by commerce itself.

APPENDIX.

—

A.

Whereas, the Government of Paraguay, while in a state of perfect peace with this Republic, has treacherously attacked it by force of arms;

Whereas, it has seized two national war steamers in the port of the city of Corrientes (Argentine), without warning or notification of any kind, killing many of the men, and making the rest their prisoners;

Whereas, it has opened fire with cannon on the defenseless city of Corrientes;

Whereas, it has invaded by an army the province of Corrientes, occupying its capital and part of its territory;

     *   *   *   *   *   * And, lastly,

Whereas, subsequently to these aggressive acts, the Government has been apprised of the declaration of war made by the Government of Paraguay to the nation,

The President of the Republic DECREES:

1st.—That the Republic is at war with the Government of Paraguay;

2d.—That it will not lay down its arms until it has overthrown the Government of Paraguay, and obtained from it the needed reparation and indemnification, and the guarantees required to secure peace;

3d.—That the Argentine Republic, in this war to which it has been provoked, *will respect the independence and sovereignty of the Republic of Paraguay*, &c., &c.

B.

The following extracts we take from a pamphlet registry of orders found in the Paraguayan encampment at Cumbarity; it comprises the time from the 8th of January to the 14th of December, 1868.

This pamphlet, called the "Testimony of written orders issued to the bureau of the Commander-in-chief," contains 52 pages of foolscap, folded lengthwise, and is nearly all in the same handwriting. It is entirely authentic, and was sent to the imperial Government by the Brazilian Commander-in-chief.

This document has served to remove whatever doubt may still exist as to the veracity of the reports circulated as to the great number of victims, both native of Paraguay and foreigners, immolated to gloat the appetite for slaughter of the despot of Paraguay.

The detailed names of the victims put to death will be there found from day to day; the manner of that death being specified, whether from being lanced, shot, tortured, or confinement in dungeons. (*)

EXTRACTS FROM A REGISTER OF ORDERS FOUND AT
CUMBARITY.

PASO PUCÚ, *January* 31, 1868.—By supreme order, Captain Zacarias Mendoza is suspended from his rank and is to do duty as ensign of battalion 48.

(*) The accompanying list comprises but a part of the victims immolated by the cruel Lopez in his frustrated ambition for conquest. Pretending to punish a conspiracy, he has sacrificed natives as well as foreigners, in fact, every person of high standing within his reach. From such horrible acts we deduce the following dilemma: Either the conspiracy never existed (as we realy believe), or, if any, its extensiveness proves in a convincing manner the unpopularity of Lopez's cause, against which every conspicuous man had pronounced.

Lieutenant De la Cruz Campos is degraded to sargeant, to do duty in battalion 42.

Ensign Marcial Romero is suspended from his rank and to act as sargeant in regiment 21.

Ensign Thomas Espinola is degraded to sargeant.

Ensigns Sálvador Asaz and Marco Veron are suspended from their grades and to act as sargeants in battalions 40 and 41.

First Sargeant Luis Rodriguez is degraded to second sargeant, and after receiving 50 lashes will return to his corps.

Private Ignacio Cabañas will be executed.

FRANCISCO Y. RESQUIN.

ENCAMPMENT AT SAN FERNANDO, *May* 31, 1868.—By supreme command the deserters Domingo Caballero and Juan Lopez, soldiers of battalion 13, captured in the woods (the former having two wounds, one inflicted by himself and the other by his captors), will be executed in Villa Franca.

June 17.—By supreme command, the spy of the enemy, the Brazilian Juan de Silva, was executed. Also, for desertion, the artilleryman from Tebicuary, José Delvalle.

June 19.—The traitor Silvestre Silva died ; his death was a natural one.

Also, by supreme command, the following traitors from the capital were executed : Esteban Homem, Vicente Cabrera, Apolinario Diaz, Nicolas Medina, Gregorio Ferreira, and Feliz Diaz.

June 22.—By superior order, the deserter Antonio Bobadilla, of battalion 43, was executed.

Also, by supreme order, the following traitors from the capital were executed : Juan Benitez, Antonio Barbosa, Francisco Peveira, Pio Ayala, Bernardo Pereira, Dionisio Gonzales, and José Delvane.

June 23.—By supreme order were executed in irons the traitors Zoilo Diaz, Domingo Talavera, Bartolomé Mayo, Gaspar Morinigo, Miguel Gimenez, Tomas Vazquez, José Maria Quintana, and German Egusquiza, all brought from the capital.

June 28.—By supreme order were executed the accused traitors Vicente Ortigoza, Tomas Pedroza, Eugenio Caceres, Martin Morales, Tomas Cardozo, Galo Iturbe, José Manuel Otazie, and Vicente Lopez, all brought from the capital. Died, of natural death, in prison, the Brazilian deserter Pedro Antonio Alves.

July 1.—By supreme order, the deserter Victoriano Zarate, of the corps of scouts, was executed.

July 5.—Died of natural death, in prison, the accused traitor ex-Lieutenant Colonel Juan Gomez ; also the, accused traitor Sotero Torres, cavalry soldier.

July 6.—By supreme order, the deserter Eugenio Nuñez, soldier of regiment 19, was executed.

July 7.—Died of natural death in irons, the accused Emilio Neumann, a German, from Hamburg.

July 9.—Died of natural death, in irons, the accused Pablo Beccari, an Italian; also, by supreme order, the deserter Basilio Rivarola, of battalion 23, was executed.

July 13.—By supreme order were executed the following accused traitors : Juan Bautista Lescano, Marcelino Marque, Salvador Martinez, Zacarias Pereira, José Ignacio Garay, Manuel Cardoza, José Tomas Martinez, Serapio Escobar, Roman Insfrau, Juan de la Cruz Vera, Manuel Viera, Corporal Angel Alderete, Basilio Villalva, Nemesio Benitez, José Luis Botella, Manuel Montero Braga, Francisco Magallanes, Antonio Carlos da Oliveira, and Julio Bautista Dacosta.

July 14.—By supreme command, the accused traitor cavalry ensign, Miguel Gayozo was executed.

July. 15.—Died, the accused traitor Juan Lenzi Colonna, an Englishman. Died, the accused traitor Manuel Madruga, a Portuguese. Died, the accused traitor Policarpo Garro, a Paraguayan. Died, the accused traitor Trifon Cañete, a Paraguayan.

July 16.—Died, the accused traitor Buenaventura Caceras, a Paraguayan. The accused traitor Miguel Antonio Elorday, junior, a Paraguayan, was executed.

July 17.—Died, the accused traitor Manuel Bocanegra, an Italian. Died, the accused traitor José Bedoya, a Correntine.

July 18.—The accused traitor Thomas Pisarrello was executed. The accused traitor Gregorio Escobedo was executed.

July 19.—Died, the accused traitor Isidora Troche, a Paraguayan. Died, the accused traitor Domingo Pomiers.

July 20.—Died, the accused traitor Miguel Berges, a Paraguayan.

July 21.—Died, the accused traitor Agustin Elorduy, a Spaniard. Died, the accused traitor Justo Benitez, a Paraguayan.

July 22.—Died, the accused traitor Clemente Veloto, a Paraguayan.

July 24.—Died, the accused traitor Raimundo Ortiz, a Paraguayan. Died, the accused traitor Esteban Luizaga, a Paraguayan. Died, the accused traitor Agustin Piaggio, Italian.

July 25.—Died, the accused traitor Carlos Urrutia. Died, the accused traitor Ignacio Galarraga, Spaniard. Died, the accused traitor Escolastico Garcete, Paraguayan. Died, the accused traitor José de C. Fernandez, Paraguayan.

July 28.—Died, the accused traitors Esteben Idedazi and Antonio Susini, Italians.

July 29.—Died, the accused traitor José Angelo, Paraguayan. By supreme order, were executed the accused traitors Santiago Ozcariz and Manuel Cabral, Paraguayans, and Candido Vasconcellos, Portuguese.

July 30.—Died, the accused traitors Bernardo Artaza and Firmin Gonzalez, Paraguayans.

July 31.—Died, the accused traitor Francisco Rosas.

August 4.—Died, the accused traitors Manuel Coelho, Portuguese ; Abdon Molinas, Paraguayan ; and Pedro Anglade, French.

August 5.—Died, the accused traitor Sinforoso Caceres, Correntine.

August 6.—By supreme order, the criminal deserter Eusebio Herrera, Argentine, was executed ; and the accused traitor Vicente Valle, Paraguayan, died.

August 7.—Died, the accused traitor Salvador Figuerédo, Paraguayan.

August 8.—Died, the accused traitors Luciano Baez, Paraguayan ; and Juan Fusoni, Italian.

August 9.—The following accused traitors were executed : Americo Varela, Angel Silva, Antonio Airua, Antonio Tomé, Antonio Rebaudi, Antonio Guanes, Antonio Taboas, Antonio Ivala, Aristides Duprat, Baldomero Ferreira, Benjamin Santerre, Cayetano Barbosa, Eugenio Maten Aguiar, (Spaniard,) Faustino Martinez, Feliciano Hermosa, Francisco Canteros, Francisco Samaniego, Francisco Sotera, Fermin Bazaraz, Gregorio Arguelles, Inocencio Gregorio, Isidoro Arriola, José Caravia, José Valle, Juan Schamper, Juan Fusoni, (this last died a natural death a moment before being executed,) Julian Rodriguez, Julian Aquino, Duis Avila, Martin Candia, Nicolas Casales, Nicolas Susini, Nicolas Delfino, Pedro Falcon, Pelayo Azcona, Roman Franco, Roman Capdevila, Serapio Pucheta, Venancio Uribe, Vicente Servin, and Vicente Galarza.

August 10.—Died, the accused traitor Juan Padilla, Argentine.

August 14.—Died, the accused traitors Agustin Vieira and Eliseo Galeano, Paraguayans.

August 15.—Died, the accused traitor presbyter José Maria Patiño.

August 17.—Died, the accused traitors Pedro Burgos, Paraguayan ; and Coriolano Margues, Spaniard.

August 18.—Died, the accused traitor Lieutenant Juan Caballero.

August 19.—Died, the accused traitors Damasio Cuevas, Paraguayan ; and Alfredo Levreit, French.

August 20.—Died, the accused traitors Florencio Uribe, Spaniard ; and Benjamin Urbieta, Paraguayan.

August 22.—The following accused traitors were executed: Cipriano Duprat, Andres Urdapilleta, Carlos Recio, Julio Carranza, Vicente Barletto, Constantino Barletto, Antonio Oneto, Lisardo Baca, Sebastian Ibarra, Gregorio Vera, Narcisco Lascerre, Felipe Milleres, Juan Vera, Alejandro Pinto de Souza, Nicolas Jubelini, Federico Anavitarte, Tristan Roca, Benigno Gutierrez, Raimundo Barraza, Leandro Barrios, Roman Silvero, Honorio Grillo, Mateo Musó, Ignacio Ruiz, Feliz García, Feliz Arriola, Pastor Gonzalez, Juan Baeco, Juan Bautista Duré, Leopoldo Anglade, Francisco Cardoso, Miguel Lombardi, José Mino, Domingo Fernandez, Federico Gaciaga, Juan Gregorio Valle, Miguel Perujo, Manuel Espinola, Feliz Candia, Joaquin Fernandez, Enrique Tuvo, Lorenzo Graz, Francisco Molinas, Juan Andreu, Egidio Ferreiro, Desiderio Arias, José Remondini, and Pio Pozzoli. Total, 48.

The following accused traitors were executed on the same day: Francisco Rodriguez Larreta, Narcisco Prado, James Manlove, Ulises Martinez, Francisco Laguna, José Garay, William Stark, Bernardino Ferreira, José Maria Astigarrago, Leonardo Sion, Nicolas Troya, Salvador Echenique, Santiago Delucchi, Pablo Kert, José Rustei, Joaquin Vargas Aldado, Celso Correa, Domingo Rojas Aranda, Enrique García, Pilar Guaicochea, Pascual Bedoya, Juan Batalla, Juan Ferresi, Gregorio Molinas, Roque Céspedes, Marcelino Gomez, Francisco Vidal, José Rodriguez, Joaquin Romaguera, Pedro Polleti, José Maria Sancedo, José Vicente Urdassilleta, Angel Ugale, Aurelio Manchuet, Guines Ranstei, Bernardino Cabral, Faustino Rodriguez, presbyter, except Nicolas Troja, who died before execution. Total, 37.

August 23.—Died, the accused traitor Captain Roman Boga, and by supreme order the following accused traitors were executed: John Watts, Natalicio Martinez, Benigno Rosas, Luis Echevarrieta, Teodoro Gauna, Marcos Pernabe, Celestino Cattim, José Sanyur, Basiliano Lampini, Enrique Fenaus, José Haller, Charles Tevite, Alejandro Galeano, Francisco Sora, Francisco Balbuena, Bartolomé Albertoni, Esteban Meza, Aureliano Cardevila, Antonio Lucero, Melchor Costa, all foreigners, and Mariano Marques, Augustin Pires, and Manuel Fernandez, Paraguayans, the last three. Total, 23.

August 24.—Died the accused traitor Jesus Lopez, countryman. The following traitors were executed : Clemente Pereira, Martin Vera, Aniceto Duarte, Casimiro Aquino, Francisco Roman, Pablo Rojas, Miguel García, Paraguayans, and Estifanio Palacios, Juan Moreira, Maximo Rodriguez, and José Laco, foreigners. Total, 11.

August—26.—The following accused traitors were put to death : Francisco Fernandez, Paraguyan, ex-sargeant-major ; Captain Miguel Haedo, Lieutenant Anastasio Vallejos, Ensign José Villasanti, Ensign Dionisio Villalba, citizen Pablo Gonzalez, citizen Francisco Frutos, citizen Alejo Acuña, citizen Matias Montiel, Italian Siverio Bote, and the foreigners Hilario Santanna, and Antonio Fonseca. Total, 14.

By supreme order the following accused traitors were put to death : José Maria Brugnex, ex-Colonel Manuel Nuñez, Sargeant-Major Vincente Mora, Lieutenant Ignacio Ramos, Sargeant-Major Candido Mora, Ensign Rosario Bobadilla, Captain Miguel Rosas, citizen Carlos Riveros, Manuel Cespedes, ex-Presbyter Vicente Bazan, Fidelio Davila, Juan Morles, Teodoro Vera, Ensign Jeronimo Belfin, Juan Madera, Sisto Pereira, Angel Bacens, Antonio Nin Reyes, and Antonia Vasconcellos. Total, 19.

By supreme order the followiug accused traitors were put to death: Manuel Trete, Pablo Seracho, Blas Recalda, Juan Antonio Rodriguez, Francisco Decond, Valentin Bargas, Prudencio Ayala, and Valeriano Ayala. Total, 8.

ENCAMPMENT IN CUMBARITY, *September*, 4.—Died, the accused traitors Francisco Candia, Lieutenant José Martinez, and citizen Dionisio Figueredo.

September 5.—Died in prison the traitor Narcisco Nuñez, ex-justice of the peace of Villeta.

September 6.—Died in prison the accused traitors Anacleto Gonzalez, Correntine, and Joseph Font, North American.

September 9.—Died, the accused traitors the soldier Nicolas Sanabria, Paraguayan, and Timoteo Correa, Brazilian.

September 10.—Thes pies Vincente Amarrilia and Inocencio Gonzalez, Paraguayan soldiers, were bayoneted.

September 11.—Died, the accused traitors Gustavo **Haman,** German ; Lieutenant Patricio Gorostiago, Argentine ; and Antonio da Silva, Brazilian.

September 12.—Died the accused traitor Ensign **Tomas** Cespedes and citizen Roman Candia, Paraguayans.

September 13.—Died in prison, Lieutenant-Colonel Gasper Campos, prisoner of war, and the traitor, Gabriel Coria. Argentine.

List of prisoners who died on the transit from San Fernando to Cumbarity from the 27th of August to September 3.

Juan Pastore, Pedro Talena, Antonio Charman, foreigners; the traitor, Jorge Kes, Swiss; Manuel Antonio del Espiritu, Santo; the traitor, Isidoro Martínez, Mexican, José Cayetano Beurro, Carlos Bueno, Jorgé Daly, Antonio José de Mora, Pedro Lagarde, Andres Gonzalez, Eleutero Enero, Manuel Peña, José Vincente Festono, José Maria Castro, Andreas Ibanez, Bolivian traitor; Estaquio Uriarte, Manuel Rivera, Juan Almayoa, Roberto Casimiro, Valentin Blenitez, Raymundo Aquino, Manuel Borges, Miguel Silva and Ensign José Gavilan. Total, 27.

September 14.— Lieutenant Alejo Ybero was báyoneted, and the accused traitor, Naten Marischavel, Spaniard, and Carlos Moreno, Argentine, died. Colonel Bernardino Denis was set at liberty. Under date of September 4, the deserters from the enemy, the prisoners of war, and prisoners for other reasons, to the number of 190, were taken from prison to work in the trenches

September 15. Died, the accused traitors Jacinto Duarte, Parayguayan, and Balthazar de las Carreras, Uruguayan.

September 16.— Died, the accused traitors Augustin Trigo, Sebastian Insfrau, Eufemio Mendez, Antonio Ortiz, all Paraguayans, and Wenceslao José Maria, Brazilian.

September 18.—Died, the accused traitor Justo Caceres, Paraguayan. The following criminals were taken to work in the trenches: Simon da Siva, Antonio Luis de Noraes, Inocencio Monteiro de Mendoza, José da Silva, José da Costa Leite, José Justiniano, Indalecio da Souza, Manuel dos Santos, Manuel Antonio da Silva and Manuel Carneiro, Brazilians, (10 in number) and Roman Lescaro, Antonio Sanchez and Roque Sanchez, Argentines. Total, 13.

September 20.—Died, the accused traitor Mauricio Gonzalez, Paraguayan, and in his prison the Brazilian deserter, Juan Suarez de Araujo.

September 21.—Died in prison, the traitors Fulgencio Gonzalez and Antonio Quintana, Paraguayans; Justino Lescano, Argentine, and Antonio da Silva, Brazilian.

September 22.—Died, the accused traitors Francisco Pintos and José Vega, Paraguayans.

ENCAMPMENT IN PIQUISIRI, *September* 22, 1868.—By superior order, the soldier, José Segovia, deserter from the 3d regiment of artillery, captured in the district of Itá, wase xecuted. Thirty dollars reward will be given to Police Sargeant Luciano Ruydias for his zeal in capturing the deserter from 3d regiment artillery, José Segovia, a present which the most excellent Marshal President of the Republic, and general-in-chief of its armies deigned to grant him.

FRANCISCO Y. RESQUIN

September 23.—Died the traitor Sebastian Zalduendo, Paraguayan.

September 24.— Died, the Paraguayan traitor Ramon Marecos; put to the bayonet the chief of Yuty, José Lino Torres; private Dolores Caballero, Brazilian, and José Vega.

By superior order, the culprit, Lazaro Gonzalves, of Yaguaron, was set at liberty.

September 25 Died in prison, the accused traitors Juan Rodriguez, Rrazilian, and Pedro Merolles, Italian.

September 26.—Died, the accused traitor Joaquin Patiño, Paraguayan, Antonio de Souza, Brazilian, a deserter from Yaguaron, was put to the bayonet.

September 27.—Died, in prison, the accused José H. Varila,

Italian. Sent to work in the trenches the prisoners brought from Yabebiry, soldiers Deodato José dos Santos, Manuel Isidoro da Silva, and Pedro Leginaldo. Brazilians. Died, the accused traitor Focundo Salduondo, Paraguayan. By superior order the following accused traitors were put to death. Paraguayans:ex-Major Matias Sanabria, ex-Captain Ignacio Garay, ex-Lieutenant Elias Ortellado, ex-Lieutenant Francisco Sosa, ex-Presbyter Martin Serapio Servin, ex-Presbyter Juan Evangelio Barrists, ex-Sargeant Dolores Vera, Bernardo Gertellado, Gumesindo Benitez, Manuel Leandro Colunga, Zacarias Rodriguez, Vincente Dentella, Segundo Colunga, Isaac Alvarez, Francisco Ojeda, Julian Jaques, Matias Ferrera, Francsico Zelada, Daniel Valiente, José Mariano Servin, Miguel Ramirez, Jorge Centurion, José Franco, and Antonio de las Carreras, Uruguayan. Brazilians: Francisco Javier de Matos, Juan Fernandez Contaduria, José Gomez Maciel, Francisco Elenterio de Souza. Italian: Juan Beltiano, Francisco Invernisi, Juan Biaccaba, Julio Vega. Spaniards: Vicente Reina, Francisco Velas, José Maria Vilas, Enrique Reina. Argentines: Ventura Gutierrez, José Cateura, Calixto Lezcano, Juan de la Cruz Lopez, Chrisostomo Carrano. Frenchmen: Leonardo Ruz, Miguel Alderey, José Philibert. German: OctavioFulgraff. Russian: Francisco Ordano. Isidro Codina. Total, 47.

September 28 —Taken from prison to work in the trenches, the criminals Nicolas Lopez, Simon Vallejos, Correntines ; Luis Bernardo Mure, Italian ; José Maria Gomez, Santiago Romero, Justo Faria, Argentines ; Caledonio Nanua, Spaniard ; Celestino Leite de Oliveira, Francisco Joaquin, Ludovico Barraso, Brazilians. Total, 10.

By superior order, the following accused traitors were put to death : Maximo Falcon, Pablo Colman, Paraguayans ; Cecilio Vallejos, Correntine, Total, 3.

By superior order, the following prisoners were set at liberty: Presbyters Facundo Gill, and Mariano Aguiar, Paraguayans ; Sargeant Buenaventura Bordon, ditto. Total, 3.

September 28.—Died in prison, the Brazilian soldier Manuel Gonzalves.

September 30.—Died in prison, the accused traitor Thomas Gill, Paraguayan.

October 1.—Died in prison, the accused traitor, Sargeant Roque Rivas, Paraguayan.

October 2.—Died, the accused traitor Andres Garcia, Paraguayan.

October 3.—Died, the accused traitor Vicente Robledo, Argentine.

October 4. -By superior order the Brazilian prisoner of war, taken at Surubiky, Captain Joaquin Gomez Peso, was set at liberty. Died, the accused traitor ex-Ensign Antonio Santa Cruz, Paraguayan.

October 6.—By superior order the prisoners of war Sargeant Major Maximiliano Versen, German, and Lieutenant Jeronimo de Amorim Valporte, Brazilian, were set at liberty. Died, the accused traitor Marcelino Sanchez, Paraguayan.

October 7.—Died, the accused prisoner of war, Ensign Severo Gonzalez, Argentine. Died, the accused traitor Juan Carlos Lezensi, Frenchman.

October 8.—Died, the accused traitor ex-Ensign Manuel Baez, Paraguayan. Died, the accused Brazilian prisoner José Suarez.

October 11.—Died, the accused traitor José Riveros, Paraguayan.

October 12.—Died, the accused traitor Vicente Quadro, Italian.

October 19.—By superior order, the criminal traitors who deserted the flag-bearer of battalion 9, were executed; the soldier Luis Alcaraz, of regiment 30, and Ramon Paredes. Died, the accused traitor, the soldier José Palacios, Paraguayan.

October 21.—Died, in prison, the accused traitor Fernando José Moreira, Brazilian.

October 25.—Died, the accused traitor Ribeiro Costa Leite, Brazilian.

October 28.—Died, the accused traitor Thomé da Costa, Brazilian.

October 29.—Died, the accused traitor Juan Moran Bueno, Brazilian.

November 5.—Died the accused traitor Miguel Patiño, Paraguayan.

November 7.—Died, the accused traitor Benito Alvarez, Paraguayan.

November 9.—Died in prison, the accused traitors José Manuel de Campos, Brazilian; Cipriano Gonzalez, Argentine; and José Maria Franco, Paraguayan.

November 9.—Died of pestilence (cholera) in the hospital, the accused traitor Valentin Fernandez, Paraguayan Died of cholera, in the hospital, the accused traitor De la Cruz Cañete, Paraguayan. Died, the accused traitor Sinforiano Martinez, Paraguayan.

November 10.—Died of cholera, in the hospital, the accused traitor Buenaventura Blasquez, ex-justice of Carapeguà. Died in prison, the accused traitoress Maria de Jesus Egusquiza, Paraguayan.

List of criminals killed in the trenches.

Paraguayans : Mariano Lopez, Francisco Sanchez, Alejo Benitez, Sebastian Ferreira, and Buenaventura Soria—5.

Argentines: Santiago Romero, Cornelio Salazar, Luis Soto, Aniceto Chorche, José Perez, Simon Romero, Roque Mansilla, Manuel Sanchez, Angel Aguero, Cipriano Alonso, Basilio Canoma, Marcelo Herrera, José Torres, Lazaro Iarine, Santiago Avila, Andrés Atuno, Primitivo Sosa, José Montero, Manuel Alvarez, Isidoro Aguero, Lino Tarella, Nicolas Vera, Antonio Sanchez, Baldomero Artaza, Francisco Aguero, Inocencio Mendoza, Zavino Pari, Ramon Mansilla, Martin Acevedo, Ramon Perez, Celidomi Fernandez, Esteban Guanes, Maria Gomez, Juan Larrea—34.

Brazilians: José Costa, Antonio Francisco, Simon dos Santos, José Tertuliano, Manuel Sosa, Joaquin Soares, José Lucas, Vicente Correa, Lazaro Gonzalves, Joaquin de Souza, Emilio Alves, Francisco Pende, Vicente Fernandez, José do

Nascimento, Basilio Dinis, José Lautela, Manuel dos Santos, Manuel Antonio, Felipe da Silva, José Justiniano—20.

Italian : Juan Canelo—1. Total, 60.

November 12.—Died in prison, the accused traitor, ex-Presbyter Antonio Corvalan. Died in prison, the criminals Candido Centurian, Paraguayan traitor; Buenaventura Maria de Mattos, Brazilian, deserter. Died of cholera, in the hospital, the accused traitors ex-Presbyter Santiago Narvaez, Paraguayan; countryman Pedro Barrias, ditto; soldier Francisco Ensina, ditto.

November 13.—Died of cholera, in the hospital, the Argentine prisoner of war, Captain Antonio Falcon. Died in prison, the Argentine prisoner of war, Lieutenant Mauricio Soto.

November 14.—Died in prison, the deserter from the enemy, the Brazilian soldier Juan Pereira Campos.

November 15.—Died of cholera, in the hospital, the Brazilian deserter, the soldier Raimundo Coelho. By supreme order, dated the 12th, the criminal Exequiel Duré, ex-ensign of battalion 18, was executed.

November 17.—By supreme order, the accused traitor, Gustavo Guion de Libertat, Frenchman, was liberated and sent to the capital.

November 21.—By supreme order the following criminal traitors, spies of the enemy, were put to death : soldier Juan Gonzalez, of Carapegna, and Basilio Escobar.

Died in prison, the accused traitor Simon Conde, Correntine.

November 22.—Died in prison, the accused traitor, Saturnino Tavares de Silva, Brazilian.

November 23.—Died in prison, the accused traitor, countryman, Juan Cabrisa. Died, the prisoner of war, Brazilian soldier, Joaquin Manuel, Concepcion.

November 29.—Died in prison, the accused traitor, ex-lieutenant of cavalry, Eduardo Barias.

December 1.—Died, the Brazilian soldier, prisoner of war,

Francisco Juan da Silva. Died the accused traitor Vicente Gomez, Paraguayan.

December 10.—Delivered as prisoners to be conveyed to the exterior, the traitors Porter Cornelio Bliss, North American, and George F. Masterman, Englishman.

December 11.—The following criminals were put to death: Captain Andres Macial, Paraguayan traitor ; Lieutenants Francisco Ortellado, Ignacio Ozeda, Paraguayan traitor. Presbyters : José J. Talavera, Antonio Valdovinos, and Juan Arza, Paraguayan traitors. Soldiers : Bernabe Sanchez, Donato Lescano, Aniceto Coete, Francisco Sanchez, Sebastian Alonso, Paraguayan traitors. Citizens: Francisco Sanchez, Victoriano Cabrisa, Ignacio Verr, Basilio Pereira, Gasper Lopez, Eleuterio Barbosa, Luciano Decond, Simon Cespedes, Paraguayan traitors. Colonel Telmo Lopez, traitor, Argentine, from Santa Fé. Private individuals: Malaquias de Oliveira, Francisco Zalar de Oliveira, Juan A. Deante, Brazilians; José Maria Caceres, Correntine; Carlos Ulrich, Leon de Delme, French; Pedro Nolasco Conde, Correntine; Colonel Ulpiano Sotero, Correntine, prisoner of war. Lieutenants: Joaquin de Silva Guzman, Brazilian; José Romero, Argentine, prisoners of war. Ensign Pauline Baez, Correntine, prisoner of war. Sergeant Francisco Barreira, Brazilian, prisoner of war. Corporals Francisco José de Oliveira, José Francisco de Amorim, prisoners of war. Soldiers: José Barroso, Manuel A. dos Santos, Antonio Manuel Rodriguez, Antonio José da Silva, prisoners of war. Deserters: José Prucian, Francisco Tavares, (spy,) Martin Machado, Brazilians. Raymundo Ruiz, Argentine, prisoner of war. Ireneo Alvarez, Uruguayan, prisoner of war. Honorio Camba, French; José Espiritu Santo Rodriguez, Serafin Gomez de Moura, José Ferreira Brandaõ, Joaquin Gonzalves, José Tomas da Costa, Brazilian prisioners of war—total 49.

December 11.—Criminals set at liberty: Colonel Venancio Lopez and Presbyter Eugenio Bogado, attached to the staff.

December 14.—Lanced to death, the traitor Lieutenant Simplicio Lynch.

C.

A number of important papers were found in the camp of Lopez. Among them is a will of his, dated the 23d of December last, in which he appoints Mad. Eliza Lynch his sole legatee. There were found also two letters of the same date, addressed by Lopez to General McMahon, the United States Minister at Paraguay, in one of which he asks the General to undertake the duties of executor under his will, and in the other requests him to become guardian of his children, whom he confided to the General's care and protection. (*)

(*) It is not credible that the United States Minister has accepted the appointment with which Lopez invested him, in order to represent his adulterous progeny, and to administer his property, procured through treachery, as was most of the wealth that Lopez pretends to possess.

www.ingramcontent.com/pod-product-compliance
Lightning Source LLC
Chambersburg PA
CBHW021446090426
42739CB00009B/1674